*The River and
the Black Cat*

ALSO BY JAMES SUTHERLAND-SMITH

BOOKS AND PAMPHLETS

Four Poetry and Audience Poets P&A, Leeds 1971
A Poetry Quintet Gollancz, London 1976
The Death of Orpheus Words Etc., London 1976
Trapped Water Earthgrip, London 1977
Death of a Vixen Many Press, London 1978
A Singer from Sabiya Many Press, London 1979
Naming of the Arrow Salamander Imprint, London 1981
The Country of Rumour Many Press, London 1985
At the Skin Resort Arc Publications, Todmorden 1999
In the Country of Birds Carcanet, Manchester 2003
Popeye in Belgrade Carcanet, Manchester 2008
Mouth Shearsman Books, Bristol, 2014

TRANSLATIONS *(with Viera Sutherland-Smith except where stated)*

Not Waiting for Miracles Modrý Peter, Levoca 1993 (with Štefánia
    Allen and V S-S)
Slovensky balady Pavian Records, Bratislava 1995 (with Zuzanna
    Homolová)
Swallowing a Hair. Poems by Ján Ondruš, Studna, Bratislava 1998 (with
    Martin Solotruk)
An Album of Slovak Literature, Bratislava 2000
100 Years of Slovak Literature, Bratislava / Vilenica, Slovenia 2000
Cranberries in Ice: Selected Poems of Ivan Laučík Modrý Peter, Canada
    2001
The Melancholy Hunter: Selected Poems of Ján Buzassy Modrý Peter,
    Canada 2001
Scent of the Unseen. Selected Poems of Mila Haugová Arc Publications,
    Todmorden 2002
And That's the Truth: Selected Poems of Milan Rúfus Bolchazy-Carducci
    Publishers, Mundelein, IL. 2005
Dinner with Fish and Mirrors: Selected Poems of Ivana Milankov Arc
    Publications, Todmorden, 2013 (with Zorica Pavičić)
Selected Poems of Miodrag Pavlović, Salt Publications, Cromer, 2014
    (with Nenad Aleksić)
Tidal Events. Selected Poems of Mária Ferenčuhová, Shearsman Books,
    Bristol, 2018 (sole translator)

James Sutherland-Smith

The River and the Black Cat

Shearsman Books

First published in the United Kingdom in 2018 by
Shearsman Books
50 Westons Hill Drive
Emersons Green
BRISTOL
BS16 7DF

Shearsman Books Ltd Registered Office
30–31 St. James Place, Mangotsfield, Bristol BS16 9JB
(this address not for correspondence)

www.shearsman.com

ISBN 978-1-84861-583-0

ACKNOWLEDGEMENTS
Some of these poems have been published without titles in
Shearsman and *The Interpreter's House.*

A number have been translated into Slovak and have appeared in
Vertigo (Košice) and some have been translated into Serbian and
Greek and appeared in local publications and as contributions to
festivals and symposia.

Contents

Twenty Years After

It's the most baroque of times.
It's the least classical of weathers.
Nobody's been promoted;
some have gone to remote housing estates
to open cardio-vascular fitness centres.
All of us are to lose a belovéd friend
in three subsequent volumes.
In fact it's twenty-six years after
and I walk to my office beside the river.
It's rained and the waters foam with much mud.
I look at the colours and implements on the hillside.
The gardens are empty; a quince tree has been felled.
A plumpness pads past with a stopwatch in her hand.
I want to be challenged by the cardinal's guard.
Opportunity is burly although somewhere
you aren't conducting an intrigue
for the honour of the Queen of France.
Nor will I be your hapless accomplice.

Adam and Eve

Fashion is all we have to lose
while the glassware melts into bad habits.
Of course the clouds will accept no blame.
They simply sift through the textures
of what we'll never do to pleasure
inhibitions who always remark
"Luckily, we were just about to."
The black cat has hidden the Bible
because you declared you'd had enough
of metaphysics and bit into an example
of an apple I'd left uneaten.
Neither of us wish to read a digest
of complete restraint beside the roaring river.
So there you have it and my recovered sense of self.

One Small Idea

You can choose or not.
The river is memory riffling
its bed of stone and mud.
Or there's the sky that egg-shell blue
which is neither memory nor forgetfulness.
There's a hedgehog ambling across the lawn,
grey and brown with lilac haunches under its tail,
blood, appetite, prickles hardening into spikes
when it's terrified. It can scream.
The black cat is wary.
Undoubtedly there's history between them.
Desire, which recalls the future,
erects morose green shoots.

The Garden of Eden

All meaning is ahead of us.
What we've forgotten
the turbulent river whirls away
in its swollen ochre flood.
We've got the language,
we've got the language,
we've got the language,
but it's got no more memory
than a flexing muscle.
The black cat always recalls
that I trapped and took her to the vet.
Otherwise we must identify
a colour for this spring,
something between pink and violet,
a petal's tip showing
from a perennial
we didn't plant and can't name.

Art and Nature

The trees are as yet showing
only minute points of colour,
pink buds, yellow catkins, no leaf.
So the ice hockey stadium
isn't hidden by the trees.
Its walls were painted long ago
in a green thought in a green shade
unknown anywhere in nature,
likewise the stripe separating
the walkway from the cycle track
by the river, itself an olive green,
after the meltwater has gone.
A truck tyre is visible
and a supermarket trolley
pitched there by the three musketeers.
The black cat glides by on roller blades.
A biplane trails a banner in the sky,
"Do what comes unnaturally."

Propriety

All at once more considered,
more leisurely, more constructed,
over time less inspired,
less impetuous, less improvised,
the garden comes alive at appointed places,
brown, violet, pink velvet buds,
nature imitating the unnatural,
staked, pruned, espaliered,
a language on its best behaviour,
voices practising a nuance,
hands splaying their fingers to make a point,
smiles not residing in the eyes,
laughter deliberately musical,
a heart breaking with perfect manners
unlike the river unruly with melting ice
while slightly elsewhere between little
avenues of rose twigs the black cat trots
with the first song of spring in her jaws.

Dialectics

That drawing of Louie's, duck or rabbit?
It depends on your palate.
Both can be hung in the cellar
with porous walls through which
the river seeps in a wet year.
"Why introduce a subterranean metaphor?"
Louie or Fred before him might ask.
I could hang them in the open,
but then flies, the birds of the air
or the black cat would get at them.
Best to put the two lack of realities
where a slow putrefaction makes them
as tender as a romantic dinner for a threesome.
The bones and gristle could be an argument for.

The Varieties of Philosophy

The derelicts crowd together on a bench
with cigarettes and a little of what
you don't fancy at all in a brown plastic bottle.
They could be versions of the black cat possessing
a calm as if they'd been cured of something
they can't remember and certainly
the river withholds what it might have been
sidling by, mumbling its secrets.
Up river by the stone cross erected
in memory of Saint Opilec
two police wait beside a corpse
hidden under a blue blanket.
The policeman smokes, the policewoman
flips her pony tail from under her cap.
On the bank opposite to the stone cross
a girl in red pants passes carrying
her baby on her back papoose style.
Her dog runs down the bank and crouches to shit
in that delicate way dogs have
when they must do something sanitary.

Après Nous, le Déluge

Our theme is restraint,
the moon bound and gagged
a tarnished silver,
the river contained
by levees skirting
the edge of the town
where water meadows
glint with light in spring,
the river oozing
into our cellar,
a skin of moisture
peeling from the walls,
glitter on the floor
too shallow for pumps
through which the black cat
tiptoes flicking paws
in irritation.
Your manner to me
is restrained. You turn
your head away from
my kiss, your worst fears
brown stains on the walls.

Communiqué

A headless thrush brought in for breakfast,
the black cat more than usually companionable,
unseen, unheard the river conveys greetings
from the Holy Roman Empire to the court of France
despite the raucous manners of jay and magpie,
the calloused hands of the executioner grasping an axe,
a would-be lover having to comprehend that No means No
while the garden begins to flourish before its due time,
the apricot breaking out into white and pink
and you and I embrace naked heedless of the open window.

Deconstruction

Little Jacques, one of those
who niggled in the sixth form,
"How do you know you and I exist?"
and later coming up
with aporiai, the cracks
in the oak floorboards into which
winning lottery tickets vanish,
through which the river floods in spring.
What to reply to Jacques-in-the-box?
"Because the language says so."
And as for the existence
of others our speech intersects,
interweaves, interlocutes, interlocks,
intercourse with all
its exchange of fluids.
Inter, inter and as we approach
universal silence,
burnt to ash or interred,
switch language codes,
but retain resemblances
putting our last gasp
in front of the Latin.
Haa! Hinter, hinterland,
all our life put behind us,
landscape of nightfall,
violet streaked with shooting stars.
Wordless.

The Lost World

Our journey to the centre of the earth
begins without the clean-living white hunter,
without the absent-minded professor,
his devoted person-of-colour servant,
his critical daughter, virginal
obsessive cleaner of test tubes.
You require somebody who always leaves
the toilet seat down. I require somebody
who always laughs sincerely at my jokes.
The language synchronizes with the earth
and opens its golden fissures into which
we dive speaking unintelligible tongues.
Crust, mantle, magma are exposed as myths.
The river is a surface expression
of underground idioms and jargon.
The black cat frisks over continents
of extinct animal sounds to join us.

Material Evidence

The curb that laughs is moonlight on the stagecoach.
That my lips have pronounced your name
will be foretold before my birth.
Our guilts run like the Bible under rivers of silk.
All our vocabularies are unicorns
firm to the touch as radiators.
Our green desires reside in plastic cups.
Your fingertips won't be denied
their ambition to turn the pages of light.
I shamble away from my flesh into tapestries.
The impulse to make similar is overwhelming
landing on her paws with her black fur on end.
Somewhere else we've already or won't
unbutton each other's reasons for being here.
We've touched just the once the way chairs do
while language knelt quite naked and proud
in the middle of the forest.
We believe in the philosophy of sweat.

Metonym

Don't be otherwise the goldfish intimates
from the bowl, outside which are a black paw
with claws retracted tapping its base,
a black ear, an intent yellow eye
reflected in the curved unyielding glass.
We, too, can be seen in make-do mirrors,
your resistances, my nostalgia
for toffee-coloured misbehaviour and remorse.
I should take up smoking again,
something to do during a candid stroll
beside the river of card tricks.
There are other muscles to be stretched,
new caverns to be debated.
Your philosophy roller blades
on the slick tarmac path hands behind its back,
buttocks outlined in pink cotton pants.
I've decided I must inhabit
a phrase you might mutter to yourself.

Platonic

The Golden Age is once more upon us,
sunshine alternating with bouts of rain,
the black cat sheltering in the shed,
the river surly with reminiscences of the hills.
You and I, too, are fire and water,
our faces perfect shining miniatures
in drops of water, our kisses vapourising
with a tang like wine spilt on a hot stove.

Too Many of Us, Too Few

The river's too shallow to drown in
despite the local slammer, Lee Boy's
best efforts after too much wine
to embrace the moon's reflection.
Not yellow enough he claimed.
I once saw the police hauling out
a body after the spring thaw.
It even made the national news
for ninety seconds; not a poet,
an absconding convict. The black cat
at the time was six generations
of feline misbehaviour away.
The river is a daylight
work of art, only a dark canvas
unprimed at night, faintly lit by
wavering oblong emanations
from the windows of a line of flats.
Lee Boy has bad grammar, his rhymes
topping and tailing an obvious
pattern of subject, verb and object
and he despises my sunny language
which will not. Neither are we friends.
The spring river roars onwards
to join a greater, its ochre waters
now flicked by the driving rain.

Squall

Do you still deny that you're an endearment
let loose upon the landscape?
The blocks of flats have lost their reds and yellows
and their no-colour cancels out whatever season it is.
I have lost my temper I have to admit.
The black cat on the roof of the shed
lifts a paw in dismissal.
The river hisses a confession of sorts.

Old Romances

Let's not talk about cats and rivers.
They're in danger of becoming symbols
rather than domesticated predators.
Let's think in black and white,
not in colour with its full access
to the human spectrum from pain to joy.
It's all at once a more sharply defined world
where we lean stylishly towards
one another cigarettes in hand.
Somebody has just been proposed to on Waterloo Bridge.
The black cat has turned a corner swishing her tail.

The Odour of Play

The morning smells of leather and turpentine.
I hope matters improve towards evening
with a faint whiff of cinnamon.
There's enough of the dawn left to tint
part of the sky with the dark pink of your shoulder.
Later the sky will be a light blue yearning
for the transcendence to which the river whispers.
I kiss your throat.
The black cat chases herself up and down the stairs.
Shall we get up, shower and dress
or otherwise, nakedness being no constraint
on the best or worst we can do?
You hook your legs round my thighs and flay me.

Up on the Ridge

Church towers with custard yellow walls,
petrol stations of glass with red panels,
in front of them the black cat, far from home,
minces between lines of stubble
then arches before pouncing and trotting away
with something wriggling in her jaws.
The river is no more than a hairline fracture
in the bones of the day. Silence. Heat.
Your words savoured like mint on my tongue.
It seems I must renounce my impulse
to shape the void, to make something of nothing.
You've told me this simply can't be done.
So I let the void widen in me,
colourless, burning.

Transcendent

Now is never the time to delete ourselves.
Sun beams hasten us through a rosy haze
of bitter dust towards midday
when our shadows vanish into our heels.
That's why we need the black cat:
she survives as a bristle of black light
under the hibiscus while the afternoon
recovers us as ghosts of green refusals.
My hands cancel your breasts,
your mouth extinguishes my negatives.
We merge as duplicity
when the river rises from its bed
as a tower of silence and whirls southwards
until the stars decide to come out,
the glitter of what never existed.

Before We Met

You wish to live and die by the ocean.
You were absent from the drowned volcano
off the Malay coast where my father
washed blood and sand from a cut in my foot.
You were absent from the esplanade
at Bognor Regis where my mother
dragged me back as waves exploded over the rails.
You were absent from the beach at Accra
where I saw two boys on a rubber tyre
pulled out by the treacherous undertow.
You were absent from the collapse of childhood
in the dunes at Mablethorpe where I found
two naked men masturbating.
For thirty years we spoke in different tongues
until we met at Europe's furthest point
from the rasp of pebbles and hiss of surf.
The river is concentrated by the levee.
It negotiates between and perhaps
undermines clay and stone. We negotiate
between the source of what we feel
and the estuary where one of us
loses the other, between mouth and mouth,
between the word we've forgotten
and the word we'll never say to the other.
We were together by the ocean once or twice.
I've got the photographs to prove it.

Louise de la Vallière

I want the black cat to pass me
on a bicycle as I walk beside the river.
I want the language I'm in to show the effects
of the ever-changing light on the river.
I want, I want; the problems of desire
that the Sun King has at midday
at the height of summer. Louise de la Vallière,
a dark blonde with a somewhat heavy jaw,
is his to command in his grand system.
His life-world is empty of responses,
all light and no shadow, all mouth and culottes.
The black cat's furry hind legs push on the pedals,
but that's as mechanical as she gets.
Under the overhanging willow bushes
the river restores its principles of water.
I'll be conveyed hence in a sedan chair
almost fatally wounded from a sword thrust
babbling in schoolboy French having failed
to deliver a compromising letter
which will reveal everything or nothing at all
depending on whose fingers tear it open.

Delta

Somewhere in the middle of a watershed
between two great river systems
in rain forest or temperate beech wood
or above the tree line on a bare ridge of rock
there's a post with a tin cup on it and a notice
claiming the water is fit to drink
marking the spot where this compulsion
bubbles out to cascade, flow and idle
to a silting estuary with a lamp
on a post stuck at an angle into the mud.
What its function could be is anybody's guess
although the lamp comes on as the sun goes down.
For some reason I have to get there.
You and the black cat can come, too.

Water Music

Mist covers the fields with excuses.
What does the river do
except turn the pages of our dreams,
a rustle that follows us to the grave?
Are there memories which can't be traced back
to blood shed in sacrifice to imaginary gods?
The black cat scampers, a small rain cloud
across the glass roof of the conservatory,
with a thrush flapping in her mouth.
Beneath her a blue vase isn't the opposite
of what she's just refuted.
We're left with clumps of garlic stalks in our hands,
crumbs of earth clinging to bulbs streaked with pink.

Fission

We could still fall apart
through distress, ecstasy,
decay, disgust with each other,
a slow motion explosion
or rearrangement of reality.
We fall apart without reason,
the black cat's limbs padding
to the far points of the compass
all at the same time, her head
and yellow eyes turning slowly
in astonishment, her purr elsewhere.
Both of us become talking heads
whispering obscene endearments
above our coupled torsos.
The river of blood flows upwards
inside us though wordless joy.

Juvenilia

I've consulted my first poem,
Canticles of the Estuary,
written out in my best handwriting
before I could afford the Olivetti,
the ink blue as a child's idea
of the colour of a river
at least ten generations of cats ago.
Of course the poem was about sex and death,
something I hadn't experienced
and something I didn't wish to experience.
Between them and this side of life
was the dream time called true feeling.
I fall asleep in desire and wake in desire.
The black cat is turning pages with her paws.
The river shows a red and gold absence,
the sky a grey-blue lack of feeling.
You've always been the whole spectrum of presence.

The Circulation of the Blood

has just begun again like a long kiss renewed
between deep breaths when somebody I can never give
myself a chance with asks smiling why on earth I'm
waiting and I reply now I'm not on earth with
the black cat casting a multiplicity of
shadows from a number of suns, the river so
shallow its waters can't reach my knees as I flick
my wrist and cast an endless winding sentence which

Tachtics

The grammars of all our friends
have gathered on the powerlines
and the topmost twigs of trees
then ascended to inscribe
on the past or the future
various loudly twittering
four-dimensional figures,
a murmuration of syntax,
tachyons and tachyoffs,
nobody will see us coming
when we're gone and do be quick
into an ether where we've barely.
Tachyderms lift their long
hairy snouts from swamps to trumpet
the coming apocalypse.
The river suffers tachycardia
when swollen with rain water.
Tachyscopes provide no other
finding than infinity
ends neither sooner nor later.
Tachydramas are enacted
on pavements in our neighbourhood,
a couple shouting at each other
in dialect about stains
of bodily fluids on knickers
which belong to neither of them.
The black cat becomes a grin
a mile high which a gothic church
could never accommodate.
You and I interlocute
then interlock and can't be

told apart of life's simple pains
and pleasures oneself whilst
reading the inside pages
of the *Daily Telegraph*
featuring an especially
scandalous divorce's details
the assassin to leave no phrase
alive or identifiable
after forensic examination.

Radical Politics

The black cat knows all there is to know about
the four hundred thousand years before the Big Bang.
It's a pity she's so far outside language.
You've never played the violin for me.
Just the once I overhear your showing
our granddaughter a scrap of Vivaldi.
Olga! I think, but then take a linguistic turn
for the better away from ranting on the radio
and recall Toni Gramsci in pain all his life
as the black cat comes in out of the rain
and grooms her fur which settles under the forces
of gravity and a tongue with hooks
into its petty bourgeois order and shine.
Rain punctures the river surface with silvery glints,
a long cadenza of whispers and light.

Of What We Cannot Speak, But Do

It's time for beautiful disintegrations.
Colours splinter becoming motes
in the eyes of their beholders.
Louie is noting the family resemblances
of different flowers: a rose
is a lily is a chrysanthemum
is his language game.
Fred is tending to the horses
of instruction in my words.
It's pointless to ask if they exist elsewhere
when elsewhere is always here.
The river is a hyphen seeking
to join the empire of the senses
to the republic of letters.
The black cat is playing inside its own
extra-linguistic reality
if she but knew it though the disadvantage
of such self-knowledge doesn't burden a cat.
You and I put our arms around each other
and these absences of true stories and hug.
We're long past living in kingdoms of gold,
silver, bronze and iron. Instead we flicker
between screens of a world enabled
by a trace element mined by child labour
in the catchment area of the Upper Congo.

The Vicomte de Bragelonne

The young vicomte dies too early
to discover completely
the vicious employments of the tongue.
His life-world is well-spoken,
high sounding and filled with honour.
The system made him the fly
in the stoppered bottle.
We aren't expelled from paradise;
only when we speak with malice.
The vicomte loved and died
in the garden of his own precepts
and never understood that angels
are neither good nor evil
merely the flunkeys of a system.
The river rose in the garden
of Eden and preaches over
its fish traps and weirs under which
plastic bottles jiggle and bob.
The black cat, like an angel,
is beyond good and evil
with a range of signals
to show her momentary desires.
Just now she exercises her claws
on the camel rug which can stand it.
You and I embrace, perpetrators
and victims of uncountable crimes.

The Black Cat: A Motion Picture

There's nothing to compare with the unintended honeymoon that we couldn't have imagined. That's what happens when we think outside the box of premature burial. Luckily, we aren't laid to rest like Attila the Hun under the river temporarily diverted so his grave wouldn't be robbed. We only have to scrabble through a top soil of experience to emerge in the fresh air of unfamiliar language albeit inside a railway compartment with somebody who looks like your Uncle Ivan. He once turned down the opportunity for political asylum in Sweden, but decided against exile from his language and lived and died in a one-room flat where your brother and I found him four days after your last conversation with him, collapsed by his fridge with one side of his face squeezed up. At the funeral his face had been straightened into an ironical smile. One arm had partially resisted being conventionally positioned by his side in the best deceased manner and remained slightly raised as if he still wished to make an artistic point. The man in the compartment with us died forty years before Uncle Ivan.

The film that we're in is very dark in texture, a bad, but the only surviving print of a two-reeler. The black cat should never be allowed near it despite her claim on the title. The damage her claws could do!

Somewhere between Budapest and Višegrad we're forced to spend the night in a masterpiece of construction built upon a masterpiece of destruction as Uncle Ivan's double observes, a psychiatrist whom I catch touching your face while you sleep. He has an intense, and all-consuming horror of cats the villain, the owner of our accommodation, lisps before carrying his purring familiar past an earlier victim in a glass case, the psychiatrist's wife. "Are we not the living dead?" he asks and later remarks that even the phone is dead.

An organ plays. It's the dark of the moon and you're about to be sacrificed at a black mass. The psychiatrist rescues you and begins to flay the villain who, it is revealed has not only embalmed the psychiatrist's wife, but married his daughter whom he has just murdered. The black cat, sensing disaster, departs as we flee the house likewise to recover in Budapest. I read a review of my latest book; on the whole positive, but failing to comprehend the linguistic reality from which we've escaped.

We know that we can prey on others, that from time to time there are those who make monsters of us. Rivers whisper beneath our feet of the bones they hide, that there's a grand narrative to be disinterred. We've still got dirt under our fingernails.

Late Summer

On the way home the air lifts its restrictions.
The blocks of apartments are rosy
from vigorous occupation and young couples
emerge from them, arms linked, conversing
in a white and gold that won't peel off.
Even the old have managed not to for once
as the trees beside the river dispense
with a social order becoming bereft of phrase.
How will you greet me when my key growls
in the front door lock and I rustle through
like a gust of leaves? You step out of the shower
and appear from the bathroom as a cloud.
Impossible to tell water vapour from flesh,
the sound of your voice from the colour of your hair.
Somewhere on the other side of these sentences
the black cat waits yowling without grammar.

Nostalgia

Your possibilities are pearl grey,
vermilion your options.
I've always wanted to reveal
what you'd rather be seen dead in
than wearing to a party.
Historical romances
nowadays aren't what they were.
Nobody is killed with a sword.
Nobody wears silk except
as a special, private treat.
Heroes are all too aware of their place
in the great chain of non-being.
The flats on the opposite bank
of the river were made over
in tangerine and emerald
last autumn and to complete
the spectrum or colour clash
the river has never ever been blue
outside the child's drawing
I might have done with wax crayons
had I been brought up here though
might-have-beens have not infested
the black cat since we persuaded her
into a new flea collar.

Meagre Harvest

The harvester has left dreadlocks
of dark blonde straw on the round hill
which blinks in the afternoon light
like a boy-about-town who gets his fashions mixed;
military pants, hip hop on his iPhone,
tattoos and conspiracy theory.
9/11 and JFK's assassination
seem to be the only history he knows.
We don't press him on where the railway
beside the river led to seventy years ago.
It gleams like a snail trail on a path.
The cat is in black uniform once more,
mass murderer of mice and shrews,
nun very attentive to sparrows in the church,
plump girl who has yet to learn
the values of the spectrum so she can
replace her efforts to be a spectral presence.
Your breath is silver on my shoulder,
your heartbeat an argument without contradiction.

Blazon

The trees have devised an alphabet of colour.
The river nurses a favourite vowel
over hieroglyphs of shadow and small stones.
Yellow and green is the business of the day
although the black cat denies this
leaping from branch to branch in the apricot
as if blackness and points glittering
from the sunlight in her fur had nothing to do
with our language where syntax rattles its bones.
We regard and whisper nonsense
over the clauses of each other's bodies
to confirm we are landscapes within
or landscapes without, trees without leaves
or blossom, flowering heads without
petals or colour, scent the breeze has brought
from somewhere we can never locate.

Panegyric

It's your birthday!
Fifty-seven varieties of resistance
to easy answers and insincerity,
fifty-seven returns of the sun
to not quite the same place in your horoscope,
(this year you are lioness
with the seventh to twelfth of December most fortunate,)
fifty-seven varieties touches of a Chinese poet's brush
on the silk scroll of your being
outlining our apricot tree
and a song thrush stropping its beak
on the bark before pausing to sing
while the black cat regards it with desire
before chasing a never-ending tale
with glints of sunlight in her fur
before tale becomes golden legend, silver fable,
copper plate handwriting on a perfect sky.
Winter will come and chill our mood to the bone.
But it's only a diagram of feeling
not that real thing to which our breath gives life
where the river flows nearby with whiskery barbels
nuzzling the mud and gravel beneath ducks
that can't reach them upending again and again
above the casual flick of an orange fin.

Electricity

The good looks have been left out all night
and are soaked with dew. The black cat gives them
a wide berth as she vaguely recalls
that they fathered seven kittens on her
which she raised in our garden shed
and under a neighbour's wood stack.
Fred and Louie know nothing of what
good looks can get up to never
having had a good fuck in their lives.
Fred recommends approaching women
with a whip, embraces a cabman's horse
and loses his wits. Louie is gay
in the most fraught and celibate way.
You and I, as in life, are almost
in the midst of this. The river reveals
the colours of stripped electric cable,
green and yellow, brown, blue intertwined
before it discharges bliss through all of us.

The Man in the Iron Mask

The words I let slip lead inevitably
to confinement in an iron mask.
Don't be fooled by rumours that it's silk. It's iron.
My speech comes through to others muffled
by a grill and at length the absence
of toothpaste makes my words offensive to myself.
Outside the mask, pale or red bottle-nosed
imitations of my speech, lingo, parlance, patter,
jargon, slang, argot, cant, poetry,
stroll by the river, stroke the black cat who kinks
her tail wishing to be better acquainted.
Somebody who looks like an ideal of me
will take control, become the Sun King
while I breathe in and out silently commanding
two inches round my head. It's autumn.
I know the guards see a mist puffed through my visor
when I exhale my perfect sentences.

The Absent Friend

I'll introduce a new character
even though there's absolutely no reason to
in this sequence of passionate improvisation.
Neither you with your blue eyes nor the black cat
with its yellow orbs, to be precise green
at the centre yellowing outwards
like the meaning of meaning of the river's
conversation over the little fish traps
along its length until it widens
at the confluence with another, the friendship
of waters in their perpetual downward flow,
are acquainted with this character
who will be largely absent except
for occasional phone calls and more frequent
threads on social networks. He suffers,
is kind and perhaps doesn't know
the definitions and constraints of winter.

The Idea of Delhi

Let's persuade the limitations of distance
into a grimace of irony.
Rivers conform to mathematics
and cats don't and our distant friend's grin
is wholly without guile or malice
even when days are red and green all over.
Time like distance isn't a great healer,
but is the long feeler of a cockroach,
is the remorseless stealer of looks,
is a wheeler of prams full of junk,
is a devout kneeler in churches,
is a crooked dealer in reputations,
is the ultimate sealer of doom.
Our absent friend lives in a city of many colours
built beside the original that my country
razed to the ground after a revolution
whose leaders were tied to the mouths of cannons
and blown to bits as an example to others.
He's good enough not to mention this.
The black cat hasn't forgiven me
for trapping her and taking her to the vet.
You've forgiven my many falls from grace.

Routines of Light

Our absent friend is elusive.
His smile isn't the black cat's
which is the last aspect to vanish
having never existed in the first place.
She's rather more substantial,
certainly from the amount she eats
early in the morning at sunrise
when the day's colours assemble
drop by drop from light and at sunset
when the day dissembles fading
and resembling shadowy form
as the moon comes up and rides
on the river's indigo aspects.
You and I take each other apart
delicately as surgeons
conducting a major operation.

Narcissus

What is the end of the universe
doing on the river bank, one leg stuck
in the air while she cleans her haunches
her teeth nibbling out the kinks in her fur?
Everything is still just before winter.
Perhaps at our age we should stop dancing.
The river is quite unmoved and unmoving
on an olive carnival of mirrors
in which I make out my younger self,
thick curls of dark brown hair with hints of red.
You could easily come upon me
entranced by that pretty boy in the river
and psyche me out while your image remains
that taken by the fashion photographer,
the black-and-white profile I fell in love with.
It'd be difficult to look away
from the river and at each other.

The Genie and the Bottle

We and our absent friend
live in two different measures.
His is briefer and more definite,
a contrast between wine and brandy.
The black cat lifts her head and yowls
more piercingly at mention of his name.
She chirrups like a bird when I come home.
The river flows like isinglass
when I turn my attention to his prose,
beautiful spirits of carp suspended there.
"Who is this person who haunts?" you ask.
He's woven his gold thread into my carpet.
I can hear the distillate of his soul
dropping carefully into a beaker.
It'll have to be kept in an oak cask
for decades before being drunk
by a select few. In the meantime
I settle the cloudiness of my soul
with powdered egg shell, then drain off the clear wine.
In a month it'll be drunk at a wedding
with bawdy songs bellowed by the guests,
the pasteurised shop stuff having been swilled down.

A Collage for Autumn

Whatever it is, it isn't now I come
to mention what it wasn't or won't ever be,
a moment of crimson or sere leaf lost in the dark
on the road parallel to the river.
I slept my best, but it wouldn't be dreamt back
and I awoke to the absence of a friend
who may well have taken flight on a magic carpet
becoming imaginary or unimaginable
miles high in the clouds above the black cat
now the shape of a comma on the lawn's text,
the river tilting and transforming;
shiny ribbon, saw blade, garroting wire,
a hairline fracture between two realities.
I lean into images of myself
which topple into the distance until
I vanish completely while you arrange dried weeds
into a collage for our granddaughter;
a curve of wild barley, a splay of ragwort,
a chime of blue alpine harebell, a strand
of yellow loosestrife, an elegance of vetch.
Under this meadow you paste tiny paper cats.

Classical Elements

Vapours of historical fire,
a tongue of smoking water,
a sifting of the air of consequence,
gusts of the harrowed earth
all that is left of classical learning.
The black cat inspects a fiddle
for symptoms of atrocity
and decides the whole business is out of tune.
You've been at your aorist best;
something happened, it's over
and you can't tell me what it was.
Our absent friend declares a future
is necessary, the past essential.
"To live only in the present," he says,
"Is to be in constant discomfort."
The river was a deep turquoise this morning,
this evening will contain glints of amber.

Deciduous

The leaf-shedders have dropped
almost the last of their handshakes.
The evergreens assume
the reverence of grandmothers
by graves in the cemetery.
Our absent friend consoles us
for the loss of warmth and colour.
He's never troubled us
with his own griefs nor does he wish
to do so in any way.
The river reflects the bare trunks
and branches of a landscape
which is never ourselves,
which we'll never inhabit.
There's a mist obscuring the sun.
We can see its yellow disk
is unlike the eyes of the black cat.

Aide Mémoire

My day begins with one of those
conceited little notes to self,
"I must try to be funnier."
"About what?" you scrawl underneath.
All the leaves have gone from alders,
willow, beech, cherry, greengage,
save for those on the birches which
at a distance seem artificial,
a jeweller's fancy, gold leaf
tinkling on silvery boughs.
I must pluck a twig soundlessly
if I'm to reach my heart's desire.
There's not much to be done at work
with the black cat busy avoiding
any mention of useful pursuits,
the river sniggering southwards.
Was it something I said?

Lessons of History

Our absent friend has been good enough
not to complain about a history
which now repeats itself with a vengeance
peculiar to whatever creed
our birth inadvertently granted us
in the tangled web our culture has woven,
habits set in a stare of superiority
over two years of a mission
to civilize (correction, exploit);
opium, tea, gold, cotton, tiffin,
various generals Napier with
or without all their limbs. Goodness me,
all that fuss over rumours of animal fat!
Fix bayonets, charge and educate!
Alas Mr. Kipling the lesser breeds are
still accused of committing atrocities.
The river foams at the mouth with much blood.
The black cat being of Middle Eastern origin
is under surveillance. Look we have come through!
We've moved on since then. No, we haven't.

The Sepia Version

I glimpse myself running towards myself.
You, too, have cloned like a row of dolls
cut out from shiny coloured paper
joined together at the hip and fingertips.
Enlarged versions of the black cat perch
on every tree having rung the changes
through a pounce, a cluster, a glaring,
never quite a destruction though now
stately as an unkindness of ravens
while the river whispers in all the streets.
All at once a great bass tuba blast
as if from a truck en route to Turkey
and the knight of melancholy appears
on his warhorse. He lowers his visor
and the autumn kaleidoscope becomes
a vista in sepia. I stretch forth
my hand to touch your several selves
and hurtle right through myself through myself
until the brassy knight rides me down.

A City Break

The dome of the synagogue swells
above the unburnished city,
hubcap shaped or the breast of an amazon.
A sandstone gargoyle with a black crust
of oxidation stretches then bristles
before it scrambles over a roof.
This is a strange place to walk hand in hand
where the river is a languid brown film
unspooling towards the sea and the winter sun
flashes through the window of the bus,
which we catch, on to the faces of girls
and glints on their moustaches.
I'm in danger of writing on the sky
then overwriting until I bring on the night.
We need to deny the turquoise
and pink of touch, the moist lips of the model
on a billboard avid for shopping, for the void.

A Goose Story

The river hasn't become the black cat as I walk home
although it darkens after heavy rain
and swishes its tale told from many sources
to a blacker stain on the Black Sea.
I've narrated my way homewards past the wire fence
behind which Canada geese hissed at me
showing their fleshy orange tongues and throats.
The black cat stretches in perversely warm sunshine
under the swing seat in the garden.
She's not a negative to the spectrum.
There are colours we can't see and we've renounced
a binary mode of things as they are and are.
That winter sun could be her third eye
which we discuss as you peel off your fur
and bring your own absence of darkness,
a pink and white tender surface goosefleshing
with something like the scent of mint to our bed.

Lexicology

Our idioms have come home to roost
descending in a creaking spiral
of wings and cooing to bedaub the stone
of the public monuments of grave speech
with streaks of guano. Our patholects
are quite charming to the ear at first,
but later give themselves away
as a criminal argot of those
who deny any responsibility
for what flutters from their ceaselessly
working beaks; mating cries, alarm signals.
The black cat pounces delighted
she has neither beak nor language.

Apology

The black cat extends a quite delicate paw
and appears to be painting
as a cord, multi-coloured as the river,
ripples and twists in her claws.
Her face is impassive, her emotions
are the movements of her muscles.
Happiness is lying on one's side making art.
She lives without language and yet
is within language here. Why do you still weep,
your face blotchy, eyes puffed up?
Yes, I bellowed like a brute and in the morning
you led the black cat to me
as I lay stupefied by life-long failure.
We're into winter now, plain speech.
Mist blurs our syntax, slides in with our breath
and puts lime in our veins muffling
how much it hurts not to be able to reach
an exact word, to repair wrong.
Everything I've said is inadequate.
Cliché chills me. I'm sorry.

Cherry Tree

A young cherry at the side of the railway
quite bereft even of withered leaf;
trunk, main branches, side branches, twigs,
woody tendrils like a girl's hair
after close attention with a curling tongs.
The river loops and performs its liquid turns,
the black cat her non-linguistic turn, chasing
her tail, rounding upon herself
shins up the ivy on to our neighbour's
garage roof and then a stupendous leap
to the conservatory roof on which she skids.
What agility from such a plump little creature
before she passes out of view of this language.

Bistro

The black cat's become human
and inserted gleams of cobalt and pink
into the river which uncoils and ripples down her back
as she brings my beef burger.
I'm not sure I welcome her attempts
to practise her English. Her eyes are
a curious light blue without expression.
How dark and fragmented is midwinter
even when you enter the bistro soundlessly.
Outside there is a hegemony of snow
falling, each flake unique floating down
as separate myths of the self
entirely isolated before they melt.

New Snow

There's a white interval in the whiteness
that has fallen whitely while we slept.
Our red selves are wholly inappropriate
as the black cat, surely the essence
of pure heat, emerges from the shed
and makes marks upon the silence.
She regards the round god of writing
pecking at a string of bacon rinds.
We look up and discern scraps of blue
between the snow melting on the glass roof.
The river is silent, too, having become
blankness on which children are skating.
We hear the scratching of their blades
like fingernails on a whiteboard.

Solids

At an opposite, not pole or point
or location, perhaps 'at' is the wrong
preposition: so resting contrary
to this flow of movement and language
is stillness, the black cat poised upright
on the lawn between patches of snow,
an ingathering of shadow
contradicted by specks of light on her fur,
your bare hand peripheral in my vision
arranging immortelles, silver lozenges
of leaf and seed pod in a Roman pot,
the river recalled from our morning walk
as pewter and bronze polished for boys
playing hockey, their shouts falling short
of meaning before they reached us:
flow and stillness, the river under the ice,
your humour beneath your concentrated gaze.

Reactionary

The river's like the kingdom of France,
a frozen estate, having briefly behaved
the way an empire acquires a myth
which is simultaneous with a series
of events, is the series of events
it recalls, a level translucent surface
silvery at dusk on which boys play
pirouetting and reversing on the ice.
It's hardened over again after a thaw
caused great pieces to whirl slowly downstream
piling up against the banks like so many
chunks of fractured plate glass or glazed concrete.
Some of them are at least six inches thick.
Now the river seems to be a culvert
from an industrial estate choked
with the debris from a demolished factory.
The heavens have an artificial look,
black cloud obscuring the sun, but not enough
to hide light completely so the dark
changes away from the centre of the cloud
to a caramel hue then butterscotch
and at the very edge a tinsel gold.
I expect a baroque Christ to manifest
with a halo of sorts and showing bloody wounds.
The black cat stretches up against the back door
yowling to be let in displaying
the faint scar line from the incision
made in her belly when she was spayed.
She's been much more affectionate of late,
saviour or traitor, Magdalene or Milady
who'll promise all for a slice of salmon.

Negative

Midwinter's colours are brown and grey,
ice on the river polished to a half-shine
by the passionate games of boys whose boots
will be too small for them next year,
the woods on the hills shading from beige
to dark chocolate, only the black cat
a moving lack of speech mark free of phrases
until she turns a corner and so cold
it's like the times before this saga began,
before I could end, before I could, before
this frost bound landscape, a photograph print
where the chemicals unfix so hills, woods,
river, boys slide off leaving a blankness
glossy or matt according to client taste.

Last Judgement

The clouds have vanished,
a promise of angels
withdrawn overnight.
The river rattles
its metal drum,
the black cat shapeless
a live coal
with yellow embers
as radiance
falls from the air
winter sunlight
on the idea
of creation
as our heads catch fire
and we speak in tongues
of flame, then turn to ash.

The Dead Speak

The future is here, the past is here;
hear, hear the snow sliding on the roof
of the conservatory over glass
meltwater giggling in the gutter.
There has to be an encomium for this,
all the good blonde platitudes assembled
with their padded bras, beige make-up
and prize-winning collections of verse
or a letter of recommendation
to make sure the river runs
wherever a ceramic front-toothed
notion of nature and reality
intends it to, downhill all the way,
or a reference citing my decretals
and the brick wall I tried to build
around a shagged out idea of form
wherein the black cat was trapped by chance.
Goodness, the yowling! Your corpse remains
active outside on the phone arranging
a minor operation for me
while I decay into inspiration.

Man, Woman, Cat

I've always known that you aren't the river.
I've certainly never wanted you
to be the black cat.
You're the exit
to an impossibility
I'm not even a direction,
perhaps an interior. I'm this.
You could reply that I'm trying
to finish whatever is between us,
that cats are cats and rivers are rivers,
pewter and bronze are the ice-creams of choice.
Let the river pass a paw over its face,
the black cat creep over gravel
pursuing all the fish it desires,
you and I to become I and you,
a continuing
beside the river at night
still and solid as obsidian.
We don't hear its whisper at home
watching the full moon
as the black cat slinks in
to become motionless
except for minute twitches
of her ears as she listens
to a pitch beyond us.
Moonlight dabbles in her fur,
a darkness thrilled by silver.

Prešov, 17 October, 2015 – 17 February, 2016.